HACKING THE CORPORATE LADDER

My Time in Maersk GSC

Richu Biju

Midnight Sun

Copyright © 2023 Richu Biju

All rights reserved

Thank you for buying an authorized edition of this book and for complying with copyright laws.

No part of this book may be reproduced, or stored in a retrieval system, or transmitted in any form or by any means, electronic, mechanical, photocopying, recording, or otherwise, without express written permission of the publisher.

ISBN-9798393182502

Cover design by: TurboSoft Inc.

*To all those who want to be engineers, entrepreneurs
want to truly change things for the better sustainably*

The successful warrior is an average man, with laser-like focus.

BRUCE LEE, ACTOR AND MARTIAL ARTIST

CONTENTS

Title Page
Copyright
Dedication
Epigraph
Foreword
Introduction
Preface
Prologue
Here Begins the Book
Epilogue   74
Afterword   76
Acknowledgement   78
About The Author   80
Books By This Author   82
The book end here for Now   84

FOREWORD

When Richu and I started my career, we would always discuss what should be
the core essence of our work, and how long we wanted it to be, the few topics we came along with,
that have stood the test of time,
A brief list
- Having an 80-year work life,
- Being able to tap dance to work, by earning it daily
- Having a life's calling over having a job or career

The few other metrics we used to measure ourselves have been those which were already
marked by entrepreneurs before us, Jeff Bezos has this talk about choices at his alma mater.
and how choosing to do the hard things, and not depending on your gifts makes all the
difference in the larger spectrum of things.

The best part about this book is that Richu shares his failure more than talk
about his strengths and calibre, and how when those weaknesses were not addressed
created a rupture in his journey and what he had to do to rectify it, in order to not stifle
the success of others that rested in his hands, so if you find yourself thinking, "Oh this has
happened to me as well", then welcome on a ride to increase your scope of thinking and having
a bigger playground where you can run around more freely and breathe a fresher dose of air.

Other qualities that will benefit you forever
1) Being mission oriented rather than competitor oriented
2) Always keeping a Day 1, Week 1 mindset
3) Playing a long-term game

"Your time is limited, don't waste it living somebody else's life" - Steve Job.
You just need a shirt on your back, rest all can be earned, kept, protected over and over again.

-Love
Devika Mehra

INTRODUCTION

Welcome, I hope the book fulfils your curiosity to figure out what is it that I have done right or wrong, and becomes a boon in your own journey to maximize your time within the corporate world, and fills you with more purpose. The idea of this book is outlining a path you can use as a framework to build a high quality life.

PREFACE

The book came into existence when I felt there was a need for me to separate myself from the tough competition that was being created and it became necessary for me to learn from my previous mistakes and figure out what is that I would do right the second time around and what could others do to not make errors that I made.

The book gives you insights into my professional and personal life and insights into how the both intersected and how I had to navigate the pressure and stress from a high value job.

PROLOGUE

You dont need any particular core skills to understand the book but I hope you have some core aptitude and skills which you can market to help you get a highly valuable job that can further elevate your career to higher heights.
The only requirement that I feel the reader must have is to keep an open mind till the end and be able to gap bridges in their knowledge.

HERE BEGINS THE BOOK

RICHU BIJU

HACKING THE CORPORATE LADDER

MY TIME IN MAERSK GSC

Maersk

What can I say about Maersk it's been one of the biggest privileges for me to pen down my thoughts on this company the people I have had there was one of the biggest pleasures and the learning curve I had the. The failure endured you looking back have been highly painful in that makes me think twice in what I had in my hand and how I let it slip at times , but like almost all lovers who lose their love interest and reflect on what could have been done right, this could be an ode maybe for myself when I get another opportunity or maybe something others can learn from

The book entails all my personal thoughts opinions biases and lessons in the process, during this time when I got to know about Maersk and how the opportunity came to me, it was a period where I had been in a highly competitive space in my mind, reflecting first and foremost I truly believe it is one of the best quality a person can have, the ability to fight back, look at reality and fight onec more. When you lose that fighting quality or that valueable ability to not get back up again, you lose you r unique selling point in life and how you could have be a boon to society, the reason why I believe this is because every time I stopped fighting, I lost so much , I hated myself because I was not fighting, the biggest reason why I have put of fighting at times has been because I didn't want to hurt some onesomeone, this usalyyusually comes from a corporate equation where you need the relation, but looking back and looking ahead as well, I am convinced it is worth fighting all the time, and being fiercely competitive is one of the besr qaultiesbest qualities one can have it life,

The book entails a lot of subsections, idea along the way, how my opinion changed about things, how I ultimately lost something to gain something else, what was my process in the way, who were those who were most affected in the way, whose life has been impacted in a better way, but more so what the next generation can achieve, .

A bit on who I am. An engineer

I hated it , or maybe I loved it, my days in college has were a mess , there was good and bad, throughout engineering a constant cycle of yin and yan, throughout my engineering period one theme was common, I had an ex who left me for someone else after we ended thing in a couple of months, we were never compatible, never will be, but that really was the thing that ran my engineering days, and almost consumed my thought process in its entirety, . Fortunately, the moment college was over, I never had a thought off it, else I would have been worse and those troubled moments gave me new individuals whom I loved deeply.

Jan 2021

It start when I quit my job from a company where I just couldn't take on the abuses from a senior manager and boss, majorly because I just couldn't not focus on the task at hand it was against my desire to work there for such a low paid job, and listening to someone who didn't add true value to my skillset.

I tried being did my best to prove that I was good but I wasn't able to prove I was capable , majorly because software engineering was not something I naturally gravitated to , a lesson I recently learned from the 8 intelligence model from Howard Gardner's in 2023, a poster which was present in my college right from my first year in engineering , the poster repulsed me right from the first moment because of it colour and attitude to teach, and me being someone who did not like learning ever, or giving up control at all, all these accumulated me to kind of hating college from an academic stand point, but loving the life of a teenager and what it offered to me, : tons of women.

Not diverting from the story, the first tech role I had in a company called Blue Flame Labs, had me put in a group of 34 individual inclusive of myself, and a manager kind of guy, who. The manager, a Rakesh from Rajasthan was informed I was what a great candidate I was(not a brag, being as modest as possible) and was help bent on breaking me and getting me to listen to him and follow his vision, something I never did. Three months in, one fine day after his multiple attempts to teach me something and my desire to not get along, we fought over call and I quit, the reason was pretty simple , office was 23 kms from home, I had no cash for fuel and food, I couldn't go to office, and the work wasn't done as well, so when he asked why I didn't come to office, I didn't answer him hoping to keep the lacks of money and humiliation associated with it under wrap, increasingly as time went on the dude kept rambling on me and one of the best lessons of life came along, when you don't have money you go to work with others, and eventually slowly-slowly you build the resilience to criticism and develop a better work ethic.

The major fight between both of us was for power struggle, I was, still am and never will be someone who recedes power, sure as you evolve you have to trust people to do better work and give them the power to do things better than you can and be prepared to focus on more important and pushing ideas that can help humanity in the long run.

After that I got a new job from Jan onwards I had another role, at a firm named Xpressbees I had applied for this one much more closer to home and this job was one that was really amazing in terms of the value it added to me, majorly because the people were good, it was an entire batch they hired and had freshly graduate student who were mostly a year younger than me , it humbled me in the sense that it made me realize themesthe mistakes

I had made because of all the switching around, but the pay was relatively better , and since it was closer to home, that it seemed like a good opportunity, slowly after our first week or so we were segregated into teams, truth be said I was not in the best team , mostly was around the support team and from an engineering point for view, it didn't make sense, because the learning curve was low, so I had to work extra hard to make changes, I walked to and from office, some days early morning.

Few days I had to take a rickshaw since being late was an issue as I worked till 830 pm when traffic was dwindling, and once all employees had left, I left the office premise, I'd leave for home and reach home by 10, slept by 10:30 and continued the same, it was mentally exhausting but the fun .

I had was immense, and I while I walked to office early morning I would sweat a lot which I hated , took me an hour 30 thirty minutes to reach office, but what it did was give me a sense of accomplishment and a full on focus at work, truth be said, I would have not left the company and had goals of working there for at least 2 to 3 years, which was all to be changed, apart from myself I had two girls in my team, really good individuals, pretty sure they hated me for how many meeting I took a day just to keep ourselves more accountable and not lagging once lockdown had been reinforced again, by mid -March 2021.

Our team was okayish, we were slowly slugging forward and the learning curve was there, this is where I was more introduced to elements, languages and tools like Git, VueJS, having a server and front end code running together and actually seeing a code base work and how that resulted into a web page platform that our internal teams were using, since this company was a start-up logistics company, with heavy investors backing it up with more that 5000 employees, it gave me deep insight into how logistics and technology was working together hand to hand to reduce external costs and adding profit to the business through its core logistics work, the pay wasn't as great as that my batchmates were making and that weaswas a strong driving factor for me to learnt the infamous data stricturestructures and algorithms.

For someone like me who came in from a core tech industry and had the college education of these subjects, it is expected by tech head hunters to assume that you were skilled in these two skillsets, but truth be said I was hardly good academically in college, after a set of failures and set back I was able to make something of myself in college, for which I am grateful to a lot of people. But since Data structures and algorithms were the core component of big tech companies interview process.

I was struggling, the major reason why I struggled was because I really didn't feel DSA, CP had any real world application , they are good to help you get a job, solve problems in a controlled situation and think of creating good solutions to a problem, which are qualities an engineer must have, the key is to constantly push yourself to do more think more to separate yourself from your competitors, peers and grow over time with your core capabilities.

April

My new team with the girls, was one where we understanding the system more and more, it was about getting our hand's dirty trying to write some code, make minor modifications ,push that particular piece of code to working repository, by April as we were all at home, I felt sluggishness was hitting me and my team mates, as you become more relaxed towards your work , and have a mindset of pushing things for later, and the solution to really keep this at bay is to be accountable, so with my team mates I'd keep an every hour video call so that we didn't relax or waste precious time, which would in turn help the team grow in the long run. Looking back, I do feel it was a bit barbaric and is a model which might not scale, but the effectiveness is always there, it was something my earlier hockey coach would do with us during tougher practices to keep in a stronger spirit.

Mid -April

One fine day, I had a family friend of mine call up dad for some personal need, in that moment he enquired about me and what I was doing, as he got to know about my current status, I was offered the opportunity for an internship role at Maersk, the good Samaritan in this case was one Sujith Alex, someone I had known from our church, I would often meet and hug Sujith bhaiya when we met at church, the man was always high in energy and I always felt there was something I could learn from him, the offer came to me of the blue , and to be honest I was absolutely ecstatic , majorly because the opportunity to intern at Maersk would open up new doors for me but also a lot of individuals from my college who could benefit from this opportunity and be more useful oto the company in the longer range of things. So when I first talked to Sujith bhaiya, I said "bhaiya I am absolutely grateful to you and the opportunity you are giving", but the gratitude we felt was not just limited to myself but also was an extension from my family, and relatives, iit's something we always still talk at home.

One of the major reason this was such a big thing was because only a year ago I was scrapping by, looking for jobs, asking a lot of friends, family member and corporate employees and leaders to help me out or put a word for me, and most outright rejected me and had all sorts of excuses. So, he really came down like an angel for my career and life's calling.

The first thing bhaiya asked me was for my resume to make it well and send it to him, which I countered asking "what if I had some question to him ,for the recruiter", which were basically how would the company react to employees working longer or putting more efforts than other, would they be condemned by senior leader, an issue I faced at my current organization. At this point of time I feel that I was being childish and stupid to ask such question , majorly because you are expected to do it, Sujith bhaiya himself, told me the thing he did each day was start early and finish late.

Once the resume was forwarded to him, he did forward it to his technical recruitment team who had some delay responding to it, so again bhaiya had to call them and ask them about the further procedure to push things forward. Now these may seem like small things in the larger scheme of things but it meant a lot for me, for someone who came up from so much such a higher up position in the organization. So, I did have a recruiter who sent an email to me and had a bunch of other candidates in the cc with the exam link, the exam was within the next 2 days if I can recall around on 29th April, 2021.

Now as someone who had never taken a leave from my former office, this was a bit awkward for me to take a leave, and also, I did not want to take a pay cut for the leaves, though my paid leaves remain underutilized to this day. I didn't inform my team, went dark for the next 2 days to prepare for the exams. Which is a bad policy and not something I would consider doing now.

To stay in the best physical condition and also not waste time I had the idea of walking everyday instead of going to the gym so, I would walk roughly 16 kms every days (to and fro) which later changed to more kilometres and took me roughly 2 and a half hours, the idea or framework I had in my mind at that point of time, was if I could walk these kilometres and get a lot of my work on phone then that would really benefit my overall work ethic, so I followed it, also it didn't have me going to the gym as per someone else's control or timing, and lose a sense of ownership.

To stay in the best condition physical condition and also not waste time I had the idea of walking everyday instead of going to the gym so, I would walk roughly 16 kms every days (to and fro) which later changed to more kilometres and took me roughly 2 and a half hours, the idea or framework I had in my mind at that point of time, was if I could walk these kilometres and get a lot of my work on phone then that would really benefit my overall work ethic, so I followed it, also it didn't have me going to the gym as per someone else's control or timing, and lose a sense of ownership.

Currently this framework is not one I attest to and have another model, which provide more benefits to me physically, mentally, emotional and spiritually which is something almost most men do, go to the gym, train daily, eat cleaner and be healthier which would eventually be useful in my work. The mindset or how this works is pretty simple yet one most individual don't prefer majorly because it is not directly useful in your work, when. When you train, your brain stays much healthier, sharper, though this is never followed by senior management so even the younger generation also don't follow it.

Now all this while, since I did not have a great job, I'd walk to a neighbouring tech park in Kharadi where major consulting firm ZS Associates and now almost defunct Credit Suisse is, the idea of walking over there was to bring a sense of urgency in me to be a better engineer and be able to secure a great job, which would be high paying but also come with its own costs, usually these cost are long hours, high pressure, 1 on 1 with managers, being unhealthy and not training daily which to me is the biggest red flag or something that puts fear in my life.Now all this while, since I did not have a great job, I'd walk to a neighbouring tech park in Kharadi where major consulting firm ZS Associates and now almost defunct Credit Suisse is, the idea of walking over there was to bring a sense of urgency in me to be a better engineer and be able to secure a great job, which would be high paying but also come with its own costs, usually these cost are, long hours, high pressure, 1 on 1 with managers, being unhealthy and not training daily which to me is the biggest red flag or something that puts fear in my life.

Maersk Interview Process

I spent the next two days learning what the companies interview process is like, what they ask, the total round in interviews , what was to be expected, fortunately a lot of it was discussed on online forums where I was able to build a framework around how the companies interview process when and what challenges I could expect.

With less time to prep and lots to prepare I went on a full - on spree of learning everything I can , so during the walked daily I would prep for the cognitive interview process questions, once I was home I spent time writing code and snippets as much DSA as I could to prepare in a shorter amount of time. Once the interview came in the process was divided into 3 sections, first with the cognitive ability, which include your math problems , probability, profit loss, followed with an english test with identifying meaning of the words, aptitude, reasoning, psychological reasoning were some elements of the first round

2nd round: was mostly technical questions, majorly from Java, SQL, Database, software testing-based questions were asked

3rd round: This round was majorly coding interview rounds where I had to write a function for 2 programs.

Once it's done you can either submit it before time or use it to recheck all your answers

Overall, the interview process in April 2021, was relatively easier, currently I believe it would be in similar range or format, the difficulty is hard to guess, the best thing one can do is prepare for such cases and be as ready as possible to answer all sort of googlies that can be thrown at you.

Once I cleared this the first round, my thoughts were around the fact I couldn't clear the coding round completely, so I was naturally pre-dispositioned to worries and shattering of the vision I had built.

After almost a weeks' time and a lot of worrying in between, I finally called on of the recruiters who informed me that the result should be available by next 2 to 3 days, followed which I had an interview scheduled for me with an engineering manager, which is a fancy word for a manger who is leading the engineering team with no real engineering skills. Now this might upset a lot of people but that the core truth to it.

The Engineering Manager was a lady named Aditi Jain, who

was leading the Destination team on Maersk with two sub team within, namely, team Vision and team Destination. Both teams played a major role in building and testing infrastructure for a product which was used by the customer representative team when products came into a country from its country of origin. More details discussed on what the team did later on.

The Engineering Manager was a lady named Aditi Jain, who was leading the Destination team on Maersk with two sub team within, namely, team Vision and Team Destination. Both team played a major role in building and testing infrastructure for a product which was used by the customer representative team when products came into a country from it country of origin. More on what the team did later on

Interview was scheduled around 11 am, and this was early May, the expectation and fear of not being well versed in DSA was the only though running through my mind,

the preparation remained for other technical skills, and few questions like

- what separated me as an engineer?
- what I could bring to the team, and how could I be useful?
- career objectives that I had set for myself,
- what the company was gunning for?

and how these two could work together in intersection with the team to add value to all the individual who are invested in this.

Obviously at that point I did not know all these factors, but a rough estimation of what was expected from me was there

The meeting was via zoom, the manager in this case had an LGBQT container background and I interviewed in our lower floor bedroom as it was Mid-day and sun had peaked on its ability to burn me up, the meeting started with normal formalities and nitty-gritties that follows.

(this was my managers background during the interview)

What the manager was looking was first and foremost to understand my core skillset, competencies, how I learnt , what separated me , what I had achieved and how coachable I was, and there were a lot of technical questions around the work I had done prior, and in all honesty if you are an upcoming engineering who loves building stuff and solving problems, all the preparation that you put for the interviews is really worth it, at this point, after almost 30 mins of question and f where you really show the interviewer you are a great candidate.

The interview was broken into 3 set

1) Technical, DSA, Projects: this was where question related to heap was asked, I had few questions from whichc i asked Aditi
2) Personal quests and accomplishments, values, learning process, and history of working with others
3) Analytical, Logical questions: had a question which was asked to me by few family friends from the corporate space on a late-night session,

I would recommend try solving Shakuntala Devi, atleast 2 to 3 questions daily, it will keep your brain running and also help in the interview process, I had this question on how to divide a cake in 8 using only 3 cuts.

Few questions Aditi asked me that I remember

1.How did I learn, new technologies and kept myself in the ahead of the game?

2. What was my unique quality?

3.How did I fair in my previous roles?

One it was done, the interview was over, we ended the chat and went on with our work, the overall temperature in the room as was a good one, and I felt a bit confident but never cocky, I always believed in staying as humble as possible, you don't want to rock the boats and release others fury, another element for this mindset is because you don't want to jinx anything and be as respectful for other people's role and contribution to help you be where you are.

I went on with my current organizations work, resumed with my team, and a couple of days later around 4 pm when I had my lunch and was having a heavy lunch, I got a call from a man named Deepak, now Deepak by himself is an absolute legend, I love the man to no bounds, Deepak had this highly energetic, confident and an overall positive demeanour, classic HR skills. Deepak started off by telling me who he was and congratulating me on clearing the interview rounds and welcomed me to Maersk GSC.

Deepak went on to brief me on the further onboarding process, and asked me whether I had laptop, which I didn't so. So, I was provided by a system by Maersk and had to sign a form stating the joining with the firm. The further documentation was done smoothly, one thing about Deepak that stood out, was the fact that I had sent the remaining details the next day early morning and I had a quick reply from him, which to me implied the high work ethic the company had.

An uneasiness and giving up part of my soul

There is the really good quote which says" "if it costs your peace of mind, the price you paid for it is too high" though I wanted that high salary high repute, highly reputable organization to work with and Google has always been on top of my mind, this came in as a pain point, I had been selected what I had worked for and , along with the universe universe's blessing came ininto play, with a lot of individuals guiding me was finally here, but I felt a sense of unease, a growing heaviness for the days to come I felt and.

 I knew I was receding up control for better perks. Later that night as I laid down to sleep, I had such intense burning up in my chest, a feeling I had given up my life, I felt myself being powerless, in control of someone else and letting things run over me. The good thing that carried me was my daily morning walk, that kind of put respite into my life.

 I loved sleeping early and getting up early for my daily walk absolutely, absolute alone time, just. Just me, the pitch-dark night, my thoughts and all the pain I carried. I am naturally inclined towards something else as per Howard Greene's intelligence so that might majorly be the reason for the fear and weird gut feeling I had.

My biggest uneasiness with aching any job of any sense was the fact that I was working for somebody, I couldn't outshine them, fight with them because at is core a humans and the role of the work , or strongly present my opinion: in this case having a job for my livelihood caused me to not shine bright and go through the challenges of being a true competitor and excelling in a craft which I really love, it's something I have faced in almost every job I have taken. I know I am better than what I have been offered to do, but then the idea of being lovey-dovey, playing political games is not one I enjoyed, but then to get my bread and butter I had to play along , be more flexible and that's an advice I'd give young folks as well, never lose your inner fire or values and build things step by step, you are not the first one to whom this is happening and if it hasn't happened yet, it will happen to you for sure, there is no escaping this basic idea of " Never outshining the master", often times though you may need to break this rule to excel or be more as an individual.

Resigning and joining Maersk

Once I got a confirmation on my current organization, leaving my current organization was a challenge as I had was technically in a bond with the my current organization, so I had to make all sort of excuses to get out of here safely without damaging or pulling any strings and it had to be done in a highly efficient manner. Once the salary for May was credited, I gave my resignation by early June and the process was smooth.

After my selection at Maersk, I was down with Aa viral, so I couldn't call the main man who had orchestrated the opportunity for me, so Sujith bhaiya, himself called me and asked me about the process and how things went, he gave me a brief idea on how things went, how I had to focus on my performance, to get selected and the further interview process to get selected

A few days later the system arrived, which was delivered via an external delivery partner, in a big brown carton, the moment was pretty exciting as always and once I received the item, the first thing I thought while opening the box was how will I take it back to Bangalore once the internship is done, and I moved to a full time role. The system was an i5 processor CPU with 512 SSD, a 23-inch screen and other cables, followed which I had to take an ethernet connection for stable internet.

Once the system was setup, it was time to boot in and learnt the system and learn Maersk's internal processes and functioning. A day later I got a call from Aditi asking me about the system and how was I doing so far, one of the major issues in my relation with my Engineering manager in this case Aditi was that I did not build a strong rapport with her and the team as well, looking back the core reason was I felt a sense of being more important than be a team player, also when you are young and inexperienced you tend to be more of a lone wolf, or so I say to myself ,at least to cool off my nerves when I think of it.

My official joined Maersk by 16th June, the first few step were mind numbing , I had to connect with the IT support team to help me setup up the system which was a challenge in itself, and had to do the same with my phone, which later on turned out to be a huge error on my behalf, once I had encrypted my phone and memory card to safe guard Maersk's data, I technically could not remove that memory card and transfer my files to somewhere else and my phones decryption was not in sync, which later on cost me data from almost 2 to 3 years, which in all honestly was one that had high value to me, so if you were to encrypt your system make sure you take necessary precautions to safeguard yourself protect your data.

Induction

Once we were selected for the job role (the team who gave the interview with me) we were inducted for a meet where we were told about further joining process, it lasted 30 mins and the contents of that that meeting is nothing but a jaded memory to me. This meet gave me an idea of what the new hires were like, their background, what were their core competencies to a certain but distinct level.

Another pre here meet was done but this was more diversified, in the sense that we had people from all departments in this meet, the core idea of the meet was to introduce us to Maersk and what it did, different internal teams and how each interacted, perks, compensations, external benefits the company offered like Meal card, Vaccine drive, Top performance awards, promotions, not moonlighting, intrinsic values of the company and what its soul held onto. A set of acronyms were shared that was used within the organization, most of them were from the logistics and shipping industry. This particular meet was from 9 to 6pm.

At the end of all of this a general quiz was held to check people's understanding, needless to say I didn't fare well in this, I should have paid a little more attention to the learning. Never, the less, its a good story I have now to share.

Setting up the system sent by Maersk was a challenge fortunately Aditi had assigned me a partner for the time being to help me with the onboarding process, which was a fellow named Vivekananda Pandey from Varanasi, Viveka was a smart guy though we had a competitive love hate relation with each other, I really enjoyed his company, good person and a better engineer. Viveka graduated engineering in 2020 with me and had been to Pune a couple of time for certain project and course work, so his help was phenomenal to help me setup and learn few nits and grits of the game at Maersk, once setup the next challenge was the scrum meeting where I had to meet our team.

Looking back now I understand how important teams are and how you need to be on your best foot to be useful to your team to help launch great products which are being used by a lot of people, our daily scrum was held by 1 pm since our team had individuals from UK, Poland and neighbouring European countries. Back at home our team were majorly located from Chennai, Bangalore, Mumbai and some from Rajasthan and Punjab, it was good to have a cosmopolitan environment, and since remote work was the norm more individuals kept joining it. The next day I got a chance to meet the team, introduce myself to them where I had worked previously and how the whole experience has been so far and that I had expected to meet the team.

The team was structured like this
- Engineering Manager
- Scrum Master
- Senior Engineer
- Software Engineer
- Quality Assurance engineer
- DevOps Engineer
- Software Intern

The idea of having a scrum meeting daily is to help you with you daily task so that you can delivery constantly during a project and scrum week. The idea of having a scrum meeting daily is to help you with you daily task so that you can delivery constantly during a project and during a scrum week.

June

Now during the early days of my job at Maersk I tried learning all sorts of thing getting myself exposed to as many elements as the programming world, and I would update my manager daily about it, on teams, after a couple of days she asked me to stop doing that and just focus on learning one or two tech which would be most useful so that I can learn about it in depth and this was my first time learning frameworks, understanding about engineering and software practices in depth.

So, I went on about learning unit testing and my goal was to build something meaningful and show it to Aditi, my fear or probably lack of skill and imposter syndrome was always there, pretty sure to as the one you have at google, which I had seen can really be too much and too devastating on an individual. The key to beat such feeling or believing you don't belong is to outwork your potential and give it all that you have this way you have the upper hand to excel in your craft.

The truth to me being an asshole was simple, I lived, slept, talked, breathed and died with Kobe, Michael, Goggin's, Elon and Warren Buffett, so to me the idea of being great and constantly fighting for it was the most important, now I feel I have let go of it a bit, but truth be said I am on a constant process to be more and more like them, it's just who I choose to be and commit myself to be like, nothing else in between.

My first assignment was learning codecept JS an automation tool used to loop and run certain actions repeatedly. And trust me it took me a long time to understand what I was doing over there, when Aditi asked me what I had learnt after a couple of days:

Here is how I summarized it,

I spent all my time going through the documentation and write as much of it as possible on a text editor, then by hand writing it on paper just to get familiar with the idea of how it worked and to get rid of fear of programming, which kind of had been out of touch for me.

At that point of time since Codecept JS was new there weren't much tutorials or courses I could take on to learn from and build something so that I could gain more confidence and build something real, finally I found something on very similar lines which was puppeteer, and was able to build couple of automation cases, including one where I was pulling files from local directory, downloading files from the internet and making basic change, it was magical as always to see software doing something I wanted it to do and the computer performing functions, I remember showing it to Aditi late night around 8pm, and she seemed pretty happy about, which gave me a sense of confidence I could achieve things, but it was only short lived, like I said my bonding with my manger and team wasn't the way it should have been, and I am to blamed for that, the next day during scrum when I talked about my achievement it was brushed off, the reason being for all my achievement at that point I had a sense of greatness, which might have brushed people the wrong way, obviously I have no hard feeling about it.

Teams in June 2021

As mentioned earlier my team was divided into 2 parts the vision and destination team and we helped build, test, deploy and maintained a software which was used by the customer rep teams to fill in details for materials which was imported to the destination countries, the process or software used by these were same for all the countries we served. When I started I would attend scrums for both the teams, trying to understand what they did, which went on for almost a month, this gave me exposure to how during a scrum week story points were divided and how engineers contributed by build features and testing it, how it was planned and designed by architect and what certain elements were done the way it was done by leaders higher up the tech stack of the game

Now since I worked in the Destination team I did not have much understanding of how the vision team worked and what was it that they developed, now that may seem a bit irresponsible in my part, but the reason for that is I did not have the clarity I have right now back in the day, it was all trial and error and learning in the process, once I was set into Destination team, the daily scrum master, would start o by asking us our mood and giving emojis as per our mood(fun fact: due to organizational restructure we had 2 scrum master after the first left for another role)

Our first scrum master, was a man from Chennai with a thick south Indian accent, and once attendance was done, it was majorly disclosing what impediment we had and how team mates could work together to help someone who might have had an issue, at times we needed to communicate from players (as I like to refer to them) from other team to help get some sort of permission or data which was needed further build or test as per the requirement.

Our first scrum master, was a man from Chennai with a thick south Indian accent, and once attendance was done, it was majorly disclosing what impediment we had and how team mates could work together to help someone who might have had an issue, at times we needed to communicate with players (as I like to refer to them) from other team to help get some sort of permission or data which was needed to further build or test as per the requirement.

During my initial days by June, I had been able to learn few trick of the trade from Viveka, who taught me fragments and how to setup parts of the code, common elements like, using GithubGitHub, how code review is done, how to write good piece of software.

Since the first working day for June was from 16th, the pay was for the full month and was credited a bit late by 10th July and I had my manger reach out ot me about the late payment to which I said I was alright with it as most of my energy wasn't focused in it, it was all tuned to prove to being a good engineer, rather than having an intrinsic enjoyment towards the career path.

My daily routine a that point included getting my training early morning and then starting early and staying a bit late, trying to learn the ropes of the game, one thing that effect me due to staying at home was the sleepiness I felt

Since the first working day for June was from 16th, the pay was for the full month and was credited a bit late by 10th July and I had my manger reach out to me about the late payment to which I said I was alright with it being late as most of my energy wasn't focused on it, it was all tuned to be a good engineer, and having an intrinsic enjoyment towards the career path.

The learning from time to time was understanding the fact that now I was part of a huge organization and was making a I living for myself through it, I had so much doubt if I would fit in it, majorly because my core competencies never really promoted an engineering nature.

RICHU BIJU

July

By July I was kind of getting a grip of what the team did and how it worked & who was carrying the weight of team and how people fared within our teams, I felt this was the beginning from where I had begun to disappoint Aditi, who had high expectations initially, though I can't recall all of July, it was a good period in terms of the learning I had. A lot of the code editor was setup in my system and I was implementing good code practices & learning about how the systems were built internally.

A friend's birthday & Peoples opinion of me

By 10th July, I had a close friend's birthday & I still remember Laying back on my bed after my morning training and taking a nap for some time, I was constantly asking myself where my life had been going, it was quite the talk I had with myself, by afternoon, I had planned to meet this dude & wish him, by the time I was there couple of other friends were to join as well,

Now the reason I talk about this story is the respect I had from friends, family & people, who knew me really well, it felt great, it made me continue on my path to become a better engineer and entrepreneur & honestly dream a bit about building great products which would help a lot of individuals & families.

The general step in this process of becoming a great engineer would be something like this

→ Building a lot of stuff through code

If you don't know how to code, start with for projects you would love to have as an end user to ease your life

→ Design that on paper to give you an understanding of how

the project should be like what the UI will be like and how data would transfer where it could be stored.

→ Do that over 100's of project, if you need a comprehensive list feel free to reach out, I'll be glad to share it with you.

I have shared a set of projects list you can build, towards the end of this book

what this does is open up your eyes to how things are done and built by engineers, another thing that can be done to improve your ability to have a more intuitive sense for software & engineering combined is to

Look at all the industries you know, make a list of them, E.g.

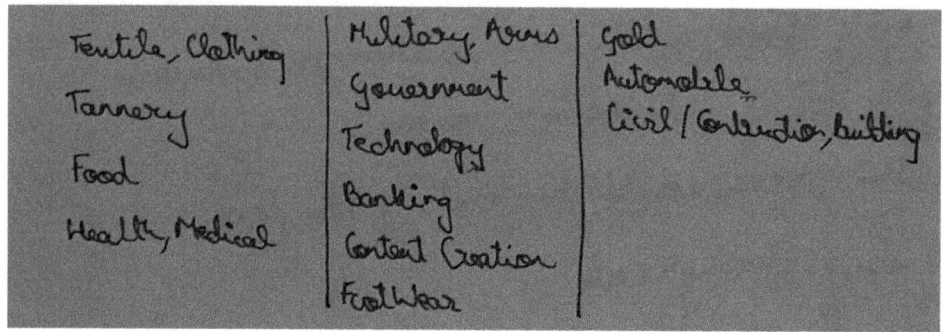

Try to take any one of the industries and think of different sectors within it.

E.g. Foot Wear

Subsection
1.Shoes

2.Sandals

3.Slippers

4.Heels

5.Flats

Once you have a basic idea

- Try figuring out how they make these products /services

-What all machinery they may need, how They are built

-And work on building software for the same, designing how your app will look and feel like, how will user be moving from one page to another and what all things it can do.

For example

Think of different parts within this particular shoe factory

→ conveyor belt

→ footwear to be printed into some mould

→ Material Needed

Once you get an idea of all items needed, you can optimize how to build you warehouse, and how the overall structure of things are within a system.

Mid-July

During July, I kind of slipped on my training, due to an illness for about 3 days especially during the covid wave, and it was a tad bit difficult to recover for me. It led me to be sick for 3 days, further making it difficult to get back to daily training and that caused me to miss training for almost 2 and a half months. That is through -> July, August, Sept.

By late September, I was able to get back to my training routine, this was particularly disturbing for me as I have always been training & eating healthier for the past 5 to 6 years, which helped my cognition and let me have more mental clarity and liveliness, which in overall, helped me gain more confidence when working, especially in a mind sport like software. One Thing I would do during my work days from Monday to Friday, was to exercise & train daily for 2 to 3 minutes for every new hour near my work station. What this did was keep my blood flowing and helped me think more clearly.

Design & Flow chart

Throughout the internship period, otherwise as well one thing we had was sessions with our design team on, who would share details on how the platform we built, was being utilized by our internal teams, in this case the end users were customer representatives and process experts who were in field to check delivery items being delivered to the imported countries ports.

The purpose of sharing the architecture of how data transferred, how internal modules were made, and how they interacted with other platforms, and what we were expected to build, In all honesty this was a great engineering practise, but it was one I could hardly understand; The presenter whose name I can't remember was too boring, so I really had to put my all into understanding what he was Trying to explain and how system worked, but more importantly how Maersk made money with it. These were usually 1 hour session every week, so prior to most of these sessions, I'd use 5 mins to bathe, meditate and be prepared for what was going to be discussed and how I could utilize it for building better services and products.

Usually, the engineering manager did not participate in it as far as I can recall, but every now and then they may drop in it to check what's happening.

Meeting the senior leaders

A couple of new hires were added to the team I was a part of somehow Aditi or the internal process team, had organized a meeting. This included our Engineering Director, Senior Executive and other top management to meet us all for 30 minutes time.

The previous day our manager had shared a document with some fancy ways to introduce us to the leader.

As the leader of "**All India Sexiest Presentation & Delivery**

Champions", the thought of using another person's PPT was disgusting to me in every sense, also the fact I could not access the link she sent me was a bonus point, So I did, what I did best, made my own presentation with Elon, Jeff resting against their rocket, my personality type as per the 16 personalities and which one I wanted. Talked more about Robert Kiyosaki and his financial quadrants & triangles, but most importantly about Michael Jordan and the earring I wore.

Now since I hadn't submitted my document, I was kept for the last to be presented, once the meeting started and the big dogs came in, Aditi set the tone for the meeting and how it was about to flow, and by the time my opportunity came, few of the top honchos had left the scene, but a few directors remained.

Overall, I smashed the presentation, it was fun and a bit unsettling to see Aditi's. face, I knew I had taken her soul, and it put me in spot light amongst senior leaders, violating the golden rule of *never outshining the master.*

August

This is my birthday month so regardless of what people say I felt great about the month and was pretty excited about it, especially this was the first one with Maersk , honestly work was getting a bit challenging and Aditi seemed to get upset about it, here expectations were dwindling and I could feel the tension in every 1 on 1 we had together every two week, she keep getting tougher and tougher, truth be said, I wasn't squat shit afraid of her, or any of the guys, there was only one truth and that was the fact that I was under Maersk's control, so I felt helpless and my desire to achieve had dwindled down tons, and as a rogue for life, I just couldn't accept the idea of working for someone and make progress. No matter how much progress I made I always knew someone was eating of all my achievement and I had to remember the holy grail of working for someone, never outshine the master, which practically said is one of the toughest things you can go through. That lack of control over my own narrative has been supremely stifling from a career stand point, I hated and still hate being under someone's control. It kills off your energy to achieve, but truth is regardless of where you are you will always have someone above you and a ton of insecurity to deal with, and slowly you develop the ability to handle criticism improved, work ethic, be able to play the game well, and build your own techniques to deal with negatives and always know that there is a black mouse in the corner to break it all down always.

Shu Ha Ri

As far as I know it is a Japanese concept for improvement in three stages of mastery and learning.

Shu: This refers to the first principle of learning your craft from the ground up, learning either from a master or by applying the techniques through self-learning.

Ha: The second stage is that of mastery, where you can control the technique, be flawless in your performance and have the ability to teach other with the highest depth and clarity.

Ri: This is where you have the skill level to break the techniques, modify it as per your needs and requirement for a particular problem set.

Jackie Chan's famed film with his teacher, "Drunken Master" from 1978 and the subsequent releases are all a great example of what "Shu Ha Ri" teaches where Jackie's teacher "Beggar so" had mastered kung fu and made his own version of Drunken fighting, which was difficult to analyse and harder for enemies to prepare for the next attacks. This was where Jackie was in the "Shu" phase of the game. This was something Aditi introduced me on our 1 on 1meeting and I was the first one she had told this to.

The idea was to be able to gauge which skills you had, and where you can radically improve, now as this was shared in a public document with our team one could be held accountable as well be able to improve their level in the game.

A sample table of how the document was and how we had to fill in where we stood.

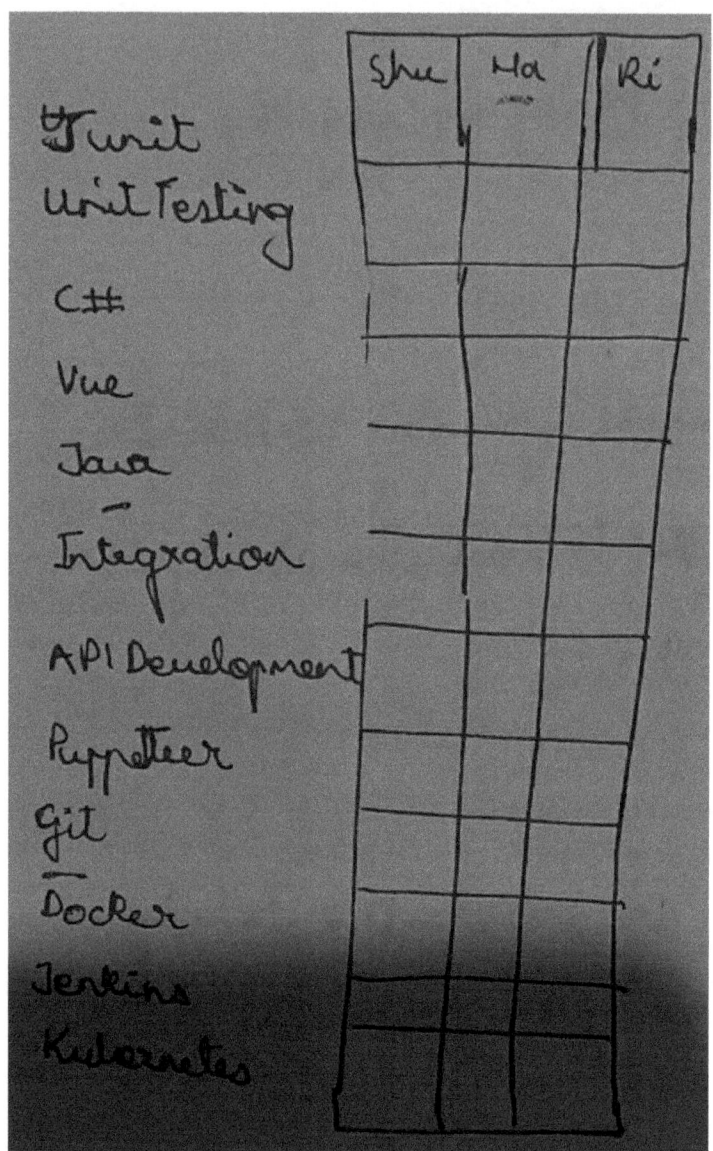

The benefit of this engineering practice was that we could

1. Identify where we were good and what needs improvement

2. For our weakness, we could learn from someone who had more exposure

3) Majorly we could assign people with projects where they have the necessary skill set and deliver projects faster and those who

want to learn had a guide to get in touch with.

Now this isn't a common engineering practice but was one our engineering manager had put in place for productivity to achieve more, and waste less.

A question that arises is how would 'Shu-Ha-Ri be beneficial in real world for our personal and professional skills. Imagine preparing for top technology companies like M·A·A·N·G ; where DSA is top priority, you could use the Shu-Ha-Ri" table to help you understand your skill level and measure your candidature positioning accurately by utilizing this chart to understand where you stand and what needs to be done to improve yourself.

	SHU	HA	RI		SHU	HA	RI
Array				Hashing			
Linked List				Graph			
Queues				Matrix			
Stacks				Segment Trees			
Heap				n-ary Tree			
Binary Tree				Trie			
Binary Search Tree				Suffix Array			
				Suffix Tree			

Mid-August

The month was a continuation of what would the events of high and lows, the learning that I remember the most were about scrum meetings. How they were held and what they represented how each sprit was planned, over time I was able to understand how scrum really worked. The model we followed was an Agile methodology with the "DevSecOps" at the heart of everything we do.

A close family friend of mine had to go to Kerala for their family reunion & wedding, and they had to leave their dog behind, as this guy was a full-grown dog. They had asked me to live in their home for 10 days or so, now I had grown up their household, so it was never a big day deal for me to stay at their place, initially I asked my mother to stay at their place, as I didn't believe it would make much sense to move all my belongings and system to their place. Finally, when the time came to move things, I took all of it and set camp there for next 10 days, my Onam (Kerala festival) and birthday: were celebrated at his place all alone, which was peaceful.

Moving to a new place meant setting up new processes and habits to live by so that was kind of a bummer, once the system was set and the family left, it was up to me to make sure my work structure remained in the right format. Truth be said, I was sleeping by 12 am and getting up day 7 am, leaving the dog out for this morning walk, poop time and then sleeping again till 9:30 then setting myself up for the day by 11 after cleaning, bathing, praying, and worrying a lot.

The first thing to do was checking on my teams emails, messages and then continue building what needed to the done as per requirement;

Further topic needs these two sub points to be better understood

- Scrum Meeting and week

-Software Setup

Scrum Week

Our Scrum cycle was for 2 weeks or 10 business days where we had to build products based on the requirement received from the development team, architects and senior engineers who had further got these requirements from the business team, inclusive of analysts, product owners, customer feedback, and new needs as per the market.

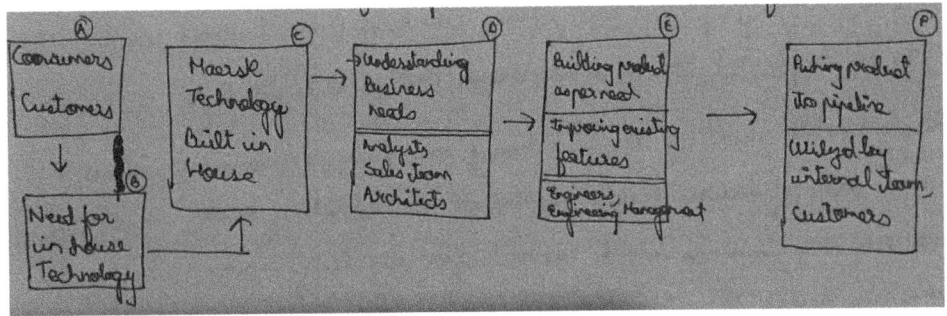

We were at stage (E) as per within the diagram, Collaboration was majorly within our community, as well as our team mates from stage D. Stage E was where all of the products were pushed into our pipeline so that they can be further used by the necessary people.

Software setup

Majority of the building of products was done in VS Code and studio which was further pushed through Git into our pipelines. The language we used was C# to build, test our back-end infrastructure, and was run using VS Studio. Reality was that I had no exposure to these and had a hard time learning it. Beginners curse. To help yourself be in a better position I recommend working on it by building as man stuff as you can and playing around with different IDE's all the time to build an internal confidence.

Resuming earlier story:

Once I was able to understand what the story point assigned to me were, I would usually try to make the necessary changes on paper and building different prototypes around it, then think of how I would write code to implement the same and bring that function to life, during my two weeks at the new house, my pair programming partner was a lady of Indian origin, settled in the outskirts of London, so to match with her time we'd connect after our daily scrum meet, plus the time she needed to settle into her work, so things would extend a little longer on my end up to 11:30pm.

It gave me ideas on how I could travel to countries apart from my own to help build a global presence for the company and also be able to see newer place and more dangerous people to meet. Things went south when the lady I was pair programming had to take her maternity leave, I was stranded all alone, waiting for a new partner, fortunately a civil Engineer turned developer took in the project and we worked to complete our task, the guy was smart and it was fun to learn how to build stuff from him.

1 on 1's

My 1 on 1's with my manager were becoming more of a chore for my manager, she wasn't getting the necessary output, and I was pissed because of the control she gripped on me, regardless of what I accomplished she'd downplay it publicly, and our relation deteriorated overtime. I remember this one particular meet we had scheduled for a Thursday, Aditi, told me about how she went about learning COBOL during her hey-day as an engineer, and how she won some sort of award, and how she would start early morning at 8 AM to outwork all, Fun Fact: these were the same qualities I told her during my interviews, as petty and funny it may sound, I could understand her game play. Instead of taking it in my stride I kind of ducked out, a bad decision from my end. Lesson learnt. ✓

By Friday my friend was back and the week was ending, by Saturday mid night I was home, setting up my system and getting ready for the week ahead. Departing away from friends is hard, especially when you are working, living, eating, sleeping, all in the same place. Next one day was about setting up myself for the week ahead and my plans ahead on getting a full-time role and also dealing with my tough relation with my manager and it was a thought I just could not get rid of. Maersk was practically in my head 24/7 every week every month, taking such a big piece of mind.

Splitting My Focus

To be really competitive & win, you have to the unidirectional and be focused on a single element to make it work in your favour. My splits were directed towards wanting more freedom, building my own business, competing at an extremely high level, thank fully none of that materialized, I was too caught up in my own head to see what was happening around me, and how I should have let go of what didn't serve my purpose.

Few things I could have done better

Personal
- Sleep well
- Eat healthier
-Tran daily
 - Meditate
- Pray daily / Gratitude
- Welcoming challenges

Professionally
- Focus on doing my work better
-Leave my ego, outside work harder

-Better relation with my manager

-Not do multiple things & Focus on full time conversion.

The platform we were working on needed multiple changes and few new features to be built from scratch, and since it was integrated with multiple other sub section of engineering team, we had to make sure that our end points were really ingesting the data we had given it, especially when we added filters to give details about where our ships / containers were headed, when would they touch their exact location, timing and other details.

Testing these were another challenge, as a highly confused individual about my career path in software engineering, it was really getting tough to build great products without any real idea of how things worked at Maersk.

September

I was back on with my training, and Maersk's office was 8.9 km from my home, so as a challenge to do more, be more driven and obsessed than all I was working with, I'd walk to office and come back as a part of my daily walking routine. The entire event was for 3 hours 30 mins, and in the walking process I'd the reading documents, code repositories, story points that other engineers from our Team were working on. What this did was give me more time to learn and grow faster as an engineer, another element was understanding how much more stuff I needed to learn and understanding code produced by other engineers.

For this during my free time and early morning walks I would take a story point that interested me and think how I would approach it, building a prototype on paper and what each feature in it would do, writing few code snippets for my approach and comparing how it would fair against other engineers work, along with the added benefit of brisk walk, it was quite a good deal. and I humbly grateful to the gods and all the stars that aligned for me.

My blue-eyed baby

Naturally one might wonder why would I share details about my puppy, but there's a reason to it. I had gotten a puppy from a close friend of mine, the first time I saw him, he was lying on the Veranda and was probably 16 to 20 days old, My friends whom I'd greet on my way to Maersk daily wanted to sell the dog, and I happened to be looking for a puppy for a long time, The pup was priced heavy and I loved this little fella so I paid what I had to, to get the little pup ,which practically could have got me two high quality huskies, he had these deep blue eyes and I didn't know his breed at that point of time.

I got him home, much to my mother's dismay, she relented later on, and the little guy was fun, my mother wanted to show him off to our neighbours and friends. After his first day with us mom took this young fella outside for him to follow her outside our first-floor balcony, I told her that he might fall down and asked her to get him in, she wouldn't agree. as soon as I walked down, towards the kitchen, this fellow jumped odd the open fence and fell down, I heard a loud thud and understood what happened, I ran to help him and as soon as I went towards him, he came running towards me with blood pouring of this body, and crying out for help, we got him into the bathroom and washed him as much as possible, but blood kept flowing, and as new pet owner we didn't know where we could find vets near by. By the time we found one, my pup was getting weaker & weaker, and after lots of frantic searching I found a vet, by the time we got him to the doctor , he was declared dead, my mother wouldn't let me take him home to bury him, she was too worried of her social status being impaired. I would have probably smacked her there itself when she asked me to throw the pup on the streets.

Burying the little guy was way to emotional for me, I couldn't stop thinking of what could I have done right to save him from falling, yet when I think of him each time, the only thought that really comes is of what he might have been like growing up. Ah……

The breed was a 95 percent pure breed Landseer with deep blue eyes, unexplainable rarity in India, let alone in Maharashtra, all this happened on a Monday morning, I couldn't work that day, and was the only time I applied for a leave. I sulked the entire day in pain. I texted Aditi, our new scrum master and another engineer about it and my leave was granted.

New team

By Mid-August a lot of our Teams were being shuffled and we had a couple of new hires and had let go off few individuals. Team changes are something one can expect at Maersk to happen frequently. But most of the time work was completed when engineers left, often times the guys who stay back with the team take on the work which is not completed or needs to be tested again. Another factor that I observed during my time there was when two of our engineers had kids, and shared the details with the team, it was great to see that being celebrated by our team.

On the technical side since our products had multiple users, was live and new features were constantly needed it was mandatory for our entire engineering and business team to meet at the end of every scrum meek, we had all of our teams come in together to show what their teams had built and how they had improved the platform or introduced new features, which was later pushed into our main pipeline, that was used by customers & internal team alike.

The thing about working for others is that you really are subordinate to them and their orders alike which is practically mind numbing. So, listening to these corporate leaders is very much similar to King - Slave relation and you got to do it to make ends meet, funny & vicious cycle of life.

With our new scrum master Neha, introductions in our daily meet were awesome along with our weekly one-hour team meets. Almost every month or so we had something called as townhall, and in all honesty I loved it, majorly because it was similar to the core element of a game called Clash of clans. Also, the idea of all individuals coming together to celebrate our achievements, failures, was thrilling, and since the company originates in one of the Nordic countries, it's was Viking like and I loved every minute. Another factor was meeting our leaders in person and understanding how they were preparing the organizations further for the next era.

One common element, I felt across Maersk was that to a certain extent the company was faceless, though there was an internal hierarchy which we could see, or even text these leaders in case of emergency, it felt a bit soul-less. September was also the month where I had planned to launch my new book, that I had failed to do earlier, a lot was my pending copyrights, printing, publishing, marketing, and splitting myself was already costing a ton, though I published it later on. On a special instance during my 1 on 1 Aditi asked me to choose between the two, I couldn't figure out what she was asking from me. She finally relented and asked me to choose either frontend or backend" by let her know by next Tuesday, immediately I relented and said Backend, naturally because that is where all the heavy lifting is done, regardless of what the front-end guys tell you, the best work or true work is done by us. We are the ones who break down complex challenges and really make things happen, "Advanced technology is similar to magic".

Remote Work

While I was interning at Maersk, peak pandemic was out of the picture, and what remained was all of us going back to our normal pre-pandemic life. And almost by the end of November (spoiler alert) the company had planned to have a mix of working from home & office. Currently (April 2023) it is split into 12-day WFO, 10 days WFH, which might eventually move towards a fully W.F.O setup. The benefits for WFH have been phenomenal, especially because we were able to access global talent, whose presence in the team was priceless, I remember having this one engineer I have mentioned earlier, named Michael Woch from Poland, dude was a phenomenal engineer, great spirit and a great confidant for me, I remember telling him I was afraid of writing code and breaking stuff, and he would show me tough love and we would spend a lot of time debugging, finding errors. We'd talk about his past, him drinking beer, and starting work by 8 and stopping exactly by 5pm. Few variations from how we have working cultures in India.

Benefits of work from home:

*The comfort of being at home & being able to do great work.

* No commute time wasted.

* Being with family & not paying expensive rent out.

Most of them are self-explanatory & don't need any special explanation, almost all of the benefits were enjoyed by me and my team at Maersk. On the other hand, for a beginner like myself at that paint it would have been way better to join directly in my office, in Bangalore, I say this because it may have worked in my favour to be more productive and to be more valuable in totality, regardless the key is being prepared for any situation.

Cons would include:

*No real connection with people.

* Longer working hours, work always extends.

*Might become more complacent at home.

It all comes down to one thing, how great you are going to be at your work.

What did I chose?

I chose being a backend ' engineer the moment Aditi asked my choice and Michael was set as my buddy/mentor guiding me through the process of writing code, building/testing items & pushing it to pipeline.

Unit Testing

Now I had no clue about these and had to start learning about testing right from scratch, and honestly it was one of the best things that happened for me, because this was where real engineering started, all the 4 years I spent in college now had real application, where what we were building actually made money! or reduced cost in some sense, and the idea of collaborating with others to make these things was just phenomenal.

How did I approach learning unit test & testing in general?

I took one amongst the many testing framework, e.g. NUnit, Junit, Selenium, in this case NUnit since we needed it for mocking few of our code, so what I did was something I generally do, I searched for NUnit on Google opened up 20 pages on it, learnt as much as I could verbally, followed by writing them all on paper and then on my computer's text editor, followed by IDE'S, after that I watched tons of YouTube tutorials and tried them. The idea was to get as much practise as possible to get rid of the fear, once that was all set, the next thing was to write real test cases for our products, I curated all possibilities tests I could prepare on paper, in plain human language, followed by the syntax for the system to understand, I wrote my scripts which I would then use to test further elements in working code, mocking all elements, then pushing my code for review.

Reviews were fun because almost all the times I could would get lots of code checks from my senior engineers, and to some extent that's majorly because engineers feel smart and powerful when they break and tear your code apart, partly it is also a useful to toughen yourself up and be willing to change and adapt as per necessity.

Another fun fact I realized is that, the longer the code written, lesser the comments, reason being that for every comment you get, there has to be a relation between modules, which means more time to check and verify all written programs, and might become a headache for the reviewer as it takes away time from their high priority work.

" **The goal throughout your career has to be focused on mastery, acquisition of skill, learning as much as you can, and being more relentless and hungrier till your last breath**". This is something I have tried to emulate in myself as much as possible, but to be honest, there are so many factors one may face when on their journey to mastery, like focusing on making more money, constant comparisons, bad managers, boredom and leaving when too much boredom strikes.

How Training helped me all together

By September I was training again daily, in that process of visiting Maersk daily, what was happening was that I felt more energetic after almost 3 to 4 weeks of continuous training. I still remember how I felt giving up my training costed me the most over the past 4 years, and once I was able to understand how much it meant to me and how having my training on a day-to-day basis, made me a much better employee (though I hate being labelled one), individual, brother, son amongst other roles.

Another secret on why corporate Individuals are fat is because there is no direct and strong incentive to be in great shape, that added with the high pressure from the organization, managing a team and delivering constantly adds to the fact why many men, give up all together on their training and their health which compounds and causes unimaginable consequence, 3 such elements I have observed over time, generally in life are:

1) Financial Education

2) STI'S

3) Health

1) Financial Education because it's one thing that's never taught in school, colleges and what we have is the lessons we have for our homes, society and the wealth cycle you are born into, and from a personal perspective if you are an employee or self-employed, then are needs to work harder to get into the big business & investment side of the game.

STI's: Now this is a taboo topic one might not want to talk about, and that further causes more complications to your life, so stay healthy and safe, and if you have any symptoms, get tested soon. For all of those tests available and if it turns out to the positive get the required treatment to make sure you are in the safer side of life, and if people have issues with you discussing them, you deserve better individuals around you.

Health: My biggest fear from an engineering stand point is the fact that since this is such a brain-oriented field, I might leave my training again and only focus on my mental faculties which can have real long term consequences over my health, and as men are valued based on: your ability to provide and be useful, and for that you need wealth, for which you need to work, and work requires you to be completely committed towards it. This is a great example of how greatness can cost you in a way that's damaging to your health.

Howard Gardner's 8 intelligence models.

The Core skills one needs to excel in software, for most roles are problem solving skills and spatial visualisation; but before we dive in deep. Let's talk about Howards model and what we are naturally inclined towards. Howard Greene was a legendary scientist, almost a child prodigy who went to Harvard at a pretty young age, and this model teaches one of the most important principles I learnt a little late at the age of 24.

1) Linguistic : Words, language
2) Logical-Mathematics : Solve problems, manipulate numbers
3) Spatial : : Visualize and manipulate objects in space
4) Musical : Understanding & creating
5) Bodily-Kinesthetics : Control and co-ordinate one's body movements
6) Interpersonal : Understand & effectively deal with people
7) Intrapersonal : Understand oneself, their emotions
8) Naturalistic : Recognize natural patterns and the world or outdoors

Now there are various intelligence model and one has to figure out themselves what they are inclined towards. From a software standpoint these models reveal an import idea, which is that certain individuals are more inclined towards the Logical-mathematical & Spatial intelligence and those who have such inclination highly benefits in this career.

For someone like myself who is not inclined towards these two core elements, life truly is a challenge, because you have to force yourself to learn the principles of software engineering and achieve the mastery you are behind.

But when you have bills to pay, a family to feed and dreams, wants, needs to fulfil, you force yourself to learn about these things and learn to be better at your craft, what this reality also does is put humility into you and give you the ability to push forward through the challenges, life will eventually press against you, an eye opener per se.

Few pet projects

As mentioned earlier while learning how to build test cases in C# Visual studio and automating few processes, I was able to build a lot of projects from the ground up, that I happened to present in front of Aditi which taught me a lot about the language and framework. I highly suggest that the best way to learn to code is through actually building something.

Automation

- Downloading file directly from a particular website

- Visiting Amazon page to check availability of a certain product which has high demand, less supply

- Putting LinkedIn profiles and getting all info directly through terminal of VS code

- Hitting all points of access for our internal system and pining error on exact location

- Search directly from terminal from websites like StackOverflow, GitHub

- Single sign on without activating google sync on

-Pulling PDF files for book which were searched through the terminal

Being able to build these products were the highlights I remember vividly from September and the value it added to my belief I could be somewhat of an engineer, and able to help others who are in their process of being a better engineer

October

This was one of my black swan months, the reason being a set of personal and professional collisions happening together, and dealing with these looking back was a personal challenge with their own exhaustion levels and the aftermath that followed. By October Aditi had an upper hand on me and if it felt as if she was dragging my soul at times. and in all of the honesty I can muster, it has nothing to do with my inability to perform, but my disgust to the fact I had less control my life, and I felt helpless and trapped, so now to make things work in my favour only two options remained (the classics)

1) Drown and die in my worries and challenges.

2) Fight my way vigorously to come on top of these challenges I had.

DevSecOps

This is where I officially started to learn the DevSecOps part of the game and was able to play around with the tools we had to monitor our application.

HACKING THE CORPORATE LADDER

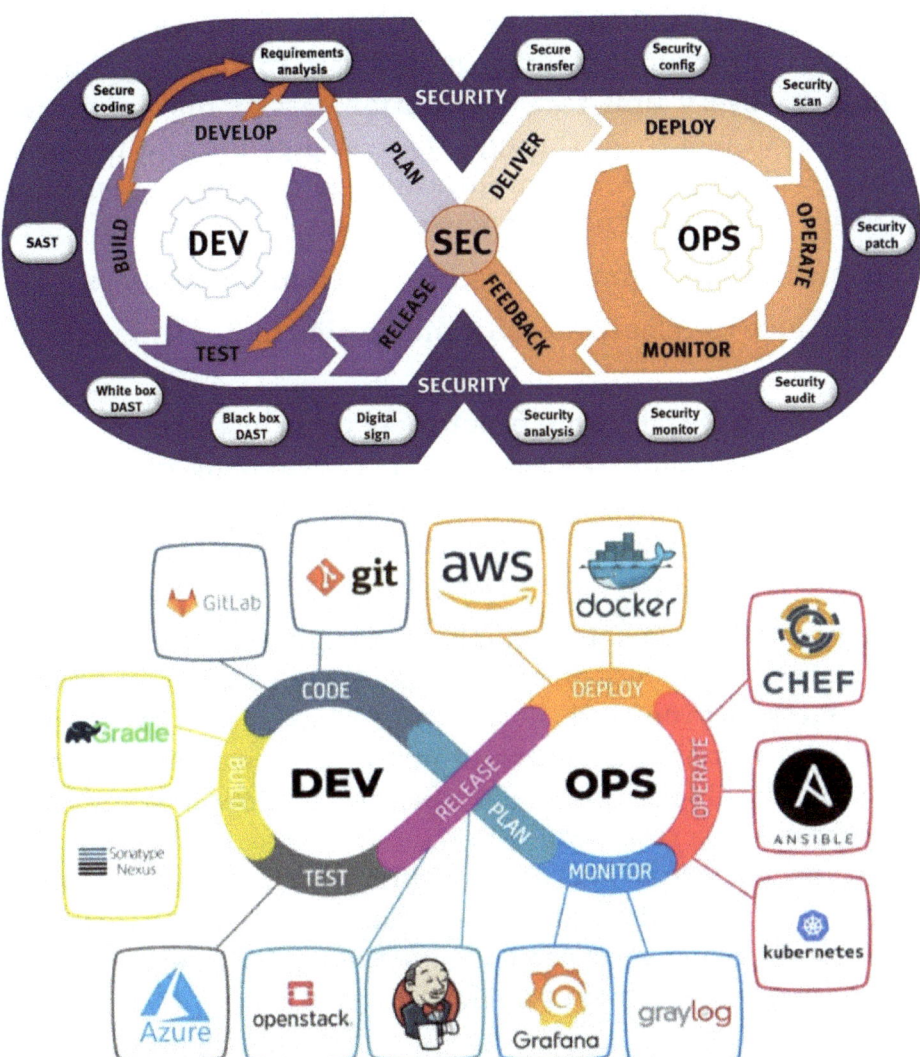

We used Azure pipelines for our continuous integrations by pushing test cases, new features, core products, and testing them constantly. Azure pipelines was something I felt naturally compatible with and gave me a strong sense of freedom, maybe because it was related to Microsoft and I trusted the engineers who worked there, the overall learning curve was minimal, few of the features I remember the most that had an impact on me was the green tick we were notified with once the pipeline successfully ran and had no break-points in them. All our builds had huge numbers and alphabets in them to give each build a unique ID, every unit test, integration test or big feature we had built all had to go through the test pipeline and it had to be made sure they were not blocking test or stopping working software. Few core benefit of Azure were,

1.Thier ability for primarily testing our running software

2. Being able to release it easily and be able to use Jenkins with it.

Kubernetes & Docker were other tools we utilized to operate & deploy our products. Docker helped in deploying our code as containers, I still remember Viveka helping me setup up Docker and I had no clue what all these new software platforms did and why we were using it.

Certainly, today after being able to design lot of pet projects and writing my own piece of software I can tell you what these elements do and how useful they are with a little more certainity, Docker for example has containers which run atop the docker engine, it isolates our application from the core host service and gives our isolated application the necessary resources like CPU, memory, network, along with giving us tools for building, managing and sharing resources. This ability to test your products within a particularly isolated environment, really makes Docker powerful.

Kubernetes

Though I did not do much work on these one of the things I learnt was how Kubernetes worked all together and the range of functions these did. Pod, Service, Deployment, Configmaps, Secrets, stateful sets, daemon set and tons of more terms from Kubernetes, have all been useful when I started learning them in depth, understanding how it was built and what is the architecture behind it and what drove it to be more commonly used than all its other competitors.

Here are some important terms related to Kubernetes:

Pod: The smallest and simplest unit in the Kubernetes object model that can be created, deployed, and managed.

Node: A physical or virtual machine that runs containerized applications managed by Kubernetes.

Cluster: A group of nodes that work together as a single system to run your applications.

Deployment: A Kubernetes object that manages a set of identical pods, ensuring that they are available and up-to-date.

Service: An abstraction layer that provides a stable IP address and DNS name for a set of pods, allowing other parts of the application to easily access them.

ReplicaSet: A Kubernetes object that ensures that a specified number of identical replicas of a pod are running at all times.

Namespace: A virtual cluster within a physical cluster that provides a way to divide cluster resources between multiple users or applications.

Label: A key-value pair that can be attached to Kubernetes objects to help organize and categorize them.

Annotation: A key-value pair that can be attached to Kubernetes objects to provide additional metadata about the object.

ConfigMap: A Kubernetes object that stores configuration data as key-value pairs, which can be used by other objects in the cluster.

Secret: A Kubernetes object that stores sensitive data such as passwords and API keys, which can be accessed by authorized containers.

PersistentVolume: A Kubernetes object that represents a piece of networked storage in the cluster, which can be used by pods to store data.

StatefulSet: A Kubernetes object that manages the deployment and scaling of stateful applications, such as databases, which require stable network identities and persistent storage.

DaemonSet: A Kubernetes object that ensures that a copy of a pod is running on each node in the cluster.

Job: A Kubernetes object that creates one or more pods to perform a specific task, such as running a batch job or performing a backup.

These are just some of the many terms and concepts involved in Kubernetes. As you learn more about Kubernetes, you will encounter many other terms and ideas that are important to understanding this powerful platform

The engineering suits

During my bi weekly 1 on 1 with Aditi, she happened to talk about how great of an engineer she happened to be and how much work I needed to do and in all honesty, it was a bit

unsettling to hear that since the image I portrayed and believed was that of someone who was willing improve, learn and be great at their craft. Honestly this hurt a bit. So, to triple down on my obsessiveness I bought two boiler suits, something manual- blue collar labours wear to protect themselves from the hard work they do and to make sure they were safe through it all. My idea of buying them and using them was since they were worn by engineers on field, If I'd be wearing them daily through my work time, I can emulate them to a certain extent, and put myself a league above all, obviously it sounded great on paper. But now I know what truly makes you a great engineer is the hours you put into your work and grow your skills over time. I had been sharing prime with a couple of close friends when they saw this, there was a lot of teasing and mocking that went on for days, which I still hear. in all honesty, their opinion stayed with me

Now I have two boiler suits in blue and orange, still in top condition, one of the worst financial decisions I made, not only did I wear it for a couple of months but, after that I had practically no real-world use of it. But what that did was give me the confidence to say to myself that maybe I can try being a great engineer to a certain extent, it all comes down to the effort you put into whatever you are doing. I still remember wearing these two oversized boiler jackets, looking myself in the mirror with the belief I could and will prove Aditi wrong.

Wedding Bell

A cousin sister of mine called me up to inform me about her wedding in Bangalore, and asked me to come join the family for the event; And naturally I wanted to be in there with all of my family so the question of how I would attend without missing my work crept it and I couldn't figure out a way to do. By early October I was convinced I wouldn't be visiting her, though a day before the wedding I cracked up, and wanted to be there with my immediate family and friends. I texted Aditi, I'd be on leave, fortunately I had no story points attached to me and it happened to be the end of our sprint run, Aditi approved it and I was off from work for 3 to 4 days

The reason I share this,

> * It's always better to plan for your events beforehand and how you would react in such situations.

> * If story points would have been attached to me, then there would have been heavy load on my programming partner.

> * Planning such leaves well ahead and delegating your work or working overtime to minimize spillage of your work is something I chose to practise now.

A family run down

As the internship was nearing its end, and my productivity had improved, phenomenally, there were some black swan moments in our household, and as a part of family, I had to take few stern decisions to make sure that things didn't take a turn for the worst, this caused me to take another days leave, fortunately Aditi was off the grid on those days as well, looking back I could have worked on those days as well and not been a wimp about things, and just worked relentlessly to make things well.

By October end a lot of the learning that I had received, had been unique in their own sense, it was not just the traditional job route of learning things, which included a blend of relationships, family, work responsibilities, failures, the rise of the younger generation and getting used to the question "Am I being average"?", "What is it that I am all about?" and then constantly trimming out efforts where it did not serve my north star.

Google x Maersk

You ask any Engineer across the globe in 195+ countries and all would love to work at Google, help build Google and grow the company as much as possible, that's the impact this trillion dollar and 25 Year old business has on the world.

So, when I was at Bangalore, naturally I had two objectives, the main one being

able to visit the Google India and Maersk business headquarters to see how the teams over there operated, what drove them, how they dressed, walked and worked, though I did not that have the permission to enter Google's premises, it was important for me to be there and learn all that I could to maximize my belief of being able to work for this firm and hopefully build great products, humanity could benefit from.

The overall experience in Bangalore is phenomenal, with so many tech companies and tons of individual from all sides of India coming in to earn a living and provide a better life for themselves and more importantly their family.

The Financial Curse

The core motivator for joining Maersk was the financial incentive, they provided along with the excitement of being in a new job, city and the people to be met there. One element I hated about being in job, and engineering college was that I was constantly being fed the idea of being an employee and not a true entrepreneur, so I had to fight everyday to keep the spirit of being an entrepreneur alive, because that is where real freedom and wealth accumulation is present.

So naturally when most individuals move towards high paying job, they don't become wealthier, but get into deeper debt, with lack of control over life and get into a vicious rat race.

A personal suggestion, I can make from my personal experience will be to save 70 percent of your salary and do that for 4 to 5 years, whilst growing your skillset and income, without getting into any debt. And utilizing all of your savings, living below your means to buy some land and build a building, which you could rent out, this way you have a second source of income.

Plan overall

- High income producing skill

- High paying job, learning the business, people and ability to make, keep and protect your money.

- Living below your means

- Buying land, building houses to rent out.

- **Real life monopoly**

Once you are able to do this for the next 10 Years, it will put you in a higher orbit of the truly wealthy individuals and help have a higher quality of life, please do not exponentially improve your lifestyle and get into debt & I request you to never get into buying any fancy things including, Clothes, Cars, Bikes, Flats to live, be bad-debt free & protect your wealth at all times.

Halting the bull

Since there was so much drama around me, Aditi was understanding of my issues and was a tad bit accommodating, but I could see the grey light amongst the cloud, the internship was about to end and the result didn't seem in my favour, I knew about this since early August, I wasn't performing like I usually did at my tasks, so this was overwhelming. At that point in time what I should have done is set clear priority on what I hoped to achieve and have a plan to reach there, but I had a loser mindset. All I had to do was take a white paper, list out why I wanted a full-time conversion, figure out the wrong doings I was on, understand what needed to be rectified and how I could have won.

I hopelessly waited for judgement day to come and was an

Aditi's strings to live my life, and as history has it, you always want to affect people's need than aiming for people's love. Once I was back from my 5-day leave, it was back to the story paints and see what is it that I needed to deliver for our partners to use.

Internal Sessions

Our core vision and destination team would have meetings to discuss newer frameworks, changes that are happening in the industry, and what all changes and improvement can be made to our existing system to make sure, we were ahead of the game all together, it would often get heated and engineers who are primarily branial creatures, and exceptionally focused on building great stuff their own way, loved an opportunity to fight over their conventions and personal idiosyncrasies. Throughout my time at Maersk, especially Mid-August onwards there were ton of meeting where Engineers would come together for these meets.

Rituals that might work

I often loved to start my work with a prayer and telling the higher power, that I don't know anything and would love to have their blessing and be able to go through the challenges and pass the needles eye. It's a practice I learnt from my friends, families and even a ton of small business owners, who would start their day with a particular routine. Now whether I am religious or not is another topic, and one off this book's context.

Fear / Back Against the wall

Somehow when everything you believed in is breaking down, and the only way is through fighting, the energy one has in them is phenomenal, and since I was going south with my internship extension, my performance with the team was top notch, and I loved it, the thrill of winning and competing lived through myself and the idea of being a software engineer, my personal way and not any other way was the truest joy I had. My relation with the team was getting much better, I kept interacting and working with most individuals to hit deadlines and actually figuring out what it meant to be a have a great career.

November

The final month of the game was here, the intense worries I had at the beginning of the month was quite a thing, I'd get up at the middle of the night, worrying what would happen next, how could I go about my career and most importantly finding a new job, which from previous experience was hugely eye opening, since I had a real tough time securing a great tech job, since my passion was never directed towards software, but I had a living to make and ends to meet. Finding a new job, clearing the interview, these were all the elements that I did not want to be a part of. By our first 1 on 1 meet for November Aditi was smart enough to address the elephant in the room, and told me right off the bat that there was a possibility that my internship would not get converted to a full-time role. After I heard it, I felt the reality slowly being absorbed into my soul, though I never reacted to Aditi's response, part of me knew the power dynamics in play and that was the core reason for our partnership to not work out, another being we were internally competing for social greatness in-essence, though she was higher up the ranks.

Once that was put aside, the only thing I asked her was if I could get a separate monitor to help me be more productive and deliver faster, to which she responded sure, "let's see how things go from here". Since my family was going through their own crisis, I didn't share any details with them, post my meeting with Aditi. Now that I had a grip over the iron knife on my head, which was if I lost this job, I knew what I'd do next.

It opened me up one of to one the most creative times I had in my life, from an engineering sense, I re-directed all of my energies to the right priority and did what was right and highly valuable.

Guts over fear

Now that fear no longer controlled my decision making the next thing, I did was get my training in the right order, I had been missing my training routine and had been on an inconsistent cycle, but the very next day after my meet with Aditi, I was back at it. Now instead of going to ZS or Maersk's office every day, I visited Pune's wealthiest man's home and that kind of set me on a new trajectory to move along.

A 2-day event

One of the unusual things that I felt Maersk had been the uncouth number of meetings we had, and for 2 days we had a session, which was just meeting with senior leaders the whole day and no work to do, I slept my way through it, because not only did these PPT guys make it super boring but were presenting in a dead way.

So, by day 2 I started attending meetings on phone, so that I could get some movement around me and get more fresher breath of air outdoors. Around 5pm I was dead sleepy and wanted a way out, so I did what the hare did and took a good nap, while the meeting continued through my phone, a while later I accidently clicked on the camera (which I held onto during my nap), and my entire team saw me sleeping.

HACKING THE CORPORATE LADDER

Suddenly I heard one of my business analyst leader Tony yell out my name, absolutely horrified and fresh of my nap, I panicked, turned off my camera and got back on track, the lesson here was to not keep my phone in my hand, and find ways to keep boring stuff interesting. I have no regrets about it though, a little fun is always appreciated.

Lesser Regret?

With my fate with the firm almost sealed, Aditi was no longer interested in the 1 on 1 and kept postponing or delaying our bi-weekly meets, and I couldn't wonder how she would react with individuals when things went south. Professionally, I had a new story point with a programming partner to complete and I focused on it.

Team's no more

By Mid - November we were informed that a lot of our team mates from different countries were being let out, mostly the one's originating from Poland were the main one's. So, I could see the core team from India was left, while most of only of us left. The morale of the team was a bit low for all of us, we had couple of games, and HR stuff planned before the final departure. Most of us had heavy load of work to the delivered, so our energies were directed towards that.

Final Call

On my last scheduled 1 on 1 meet with Aditi, she informed me that I hadn't been selected for a conversion to full time role, and she expected me to react and go crazy, I was so calm and composed through the whole thing, hardly affected by it at all; Finally we discussed what Aditi felt I could work upon to improve myself, from the whole situation, my major drawback was not being extensively hands on with software, which majorly stemmed from my fear of breaking things, and one I have been hard at work to improve, Few other details were shared as well, where I could improve myself. And then I chucked on her face before ending the meeting, walking away scott free.

A sense of pressure stayed on my shoulder as to do what next, and how life would go from there.

Reunited with Deepak

I get a message on teams from Deepak, we decided to set up a meeting the next day. On the big day, he informed me of not moving ahead with my candidature, and "relieving me", a statement that was true in every sense, my final payment would the credited once the system would be returned back to Maersk in Bangalore.

Team Reunion

Since our team was splitting completely, few final meets were held to discuss our progress at work and to acknowledge each other's time spent together, to a certain extent all of it felt made up but since we were all slaves to the system, we had to fight off this final act as well, in a "mule, weak" way.

During one of our team meets (daily scrum) Aditi informed the team that I would no longer be continuing with Maersk, and

I was busy cooking eggs downstairs, so I missed out how she informed my team about it, I kept mum towards the end of the meeting and left it once the meet was done.

Bidding Farewell

From experience I knew how the team held a farewell, which was for 30 mins for all those who were leaving, I just did not want to be a part of such a losing affair, not only did I not get converted, so now to live off my team's sympathy was unacceptable to me in every sense of the word, so I politely declined my invite, which our wonderful scrum master had organized, thankfully no such event was organized for me.

Dec 7th

By the last week of my notice period, I had completed my story points and had stopped attending meetings all together, what remained of my work was taken up by senior engineers to be completed, by the end of the day. I stopped work all together and closed the system, removed all data I had on it and was ready to roll out to a different life.

Closing Down

Now returning the system to Bangalore meant I had to pay for that cost, and with no steady income or plans to get back into the industry, I was thrifty for every buck I had, so I packed up the whole thing visited Maersk's office in Pune and asked them to forward it to Bangalore. Visiting the office premise was quite painful, to see other engineer working there and talking about things was an emotional moment for me but I had accept my hard truth and move on from there. The salary was credited a couple of days later.

Back to the Future

Once I reached home, it took me some time to reflect back on all the things that had happened and it was kind of emotional, I might have teared up a little, majorly because I lost one of the biggest Career opportunities I had. I further decided to take some time off from work, focusing on developing some real skills and getting a new job, fortunately at that point I had saved almost all of my income, so I had time and freedom to be myself. My personal suggestion to anyone in such a situation would the to take a week or two's break and get back into the industry faster.

Another opportunity

By Feb, I got a call from a Maersk personnel stating that I had been credited one more month's salary and that they wanted it back, I had no clue about this. And since all my financials were managed by our personal CA's, who further looked after our business and other interest in check, I was a bit late to revert back to the Maersk team, a week later I got a message from Deepak asking me to call him once I was free. Deepak was phenomenally great once we started our conversation around 8pm on a Monday, he further told me about the mistaken transition and further discussed about how we can resolve it, towards the end he did what all good Samaritans do, he said, "Richu, Ideally you should have been selected, but I don't know what happened, but if you are interested we have a new role in Java, based in Pune," would you be interested!", hearing this to me was gold pouring from sky right into my arms, "Absolutely" I said and an interview was scheduled next week. I thanked Deepak from the depth of my heart for his aid.

Biggest Regret

My family was living elsewhere, and things weren't going smoothly a close friend of mine had plans to leave the country, for his higher education, and this was a week before my interview.

Now the role, wasn't highly exciting, but I had to take it to support myself and make a living, the engineering manager turned out to be someone who lived 2 km's from my home, and was friends with a lot of my mutual friends and common political parties we were linked to. But the fact that the role was not as great as the one I previously had was a bit unsettling.

Now I was under the assumption I was overprepared for the role, and instead of preparing for it, I went for my buddy's farewell party, looking back I slipped one of the biggest opportunity life realistically gave me to work on and I had a heavy price to pay.

Interview Day

At that point I had no laptop, so giving the interview was a task in itself, so I went to Maersk's office hoping I could get one over there itself, I called up Deepak and asked if they could set up one for me, but that was just not possible so I joined the link through my mobile phone and gave my interview in Maersk's lobby area, which turned out to be a quiet area, the manager came in and after few pleasantries and previous experience discussion dived into the interview, around 25-30 question were asked to me within a 30 minutes time most of them being around core Java, I faired alright, though my confidence and presence might have been a meek one. Finally, once the interview was done, I left back for home awaiting an email from

Deepak, all alone while waiting for a bus to take me up.

The email came along the very next day I hadn't been selected, it didn't hit hard, then, but a couple of month later, that pain really seeped in. Then came another opportunity to re-join Maersk again, a more valuable chance.

A story for another time....................

Lessons I feel I can share

-The second interview preparation should have been done more vigorously

-Building more meaningful relations and trust

- Exercising daily and eating clean daily, sticking with a disciplined routine

-Delivering more, having a plan for 5 years and not splitting the difference

- Don't worry if you fail, keep punching ahead,

-Be truly dangerous, till the end

Projects Ideas

VueJs/ ReactJs/ JavaScript projects

1. Todo List App: Create a simple app that allows users to create, edit and delete tasks.
2. Weather App: Build a weather app that displays weather information for a user's location.
3. Movie Search App: Create an app that allows users to search for movies and view information about them.
4. Calculator App: Build a calculator app that performs basic arithmetic operations.
5. Pomodoro Timer App: Create a timer app that uses the Pomodoro technique for time management.

6. Random Quote Generator: Build an app that generates random quotes or inspirational messages.
7. Music Player App: Create a music player app that allows users to play and organize their music collection.
8. Calendar App: Build a calendar app that allows users to schedule and manage events.
9. E-commerce Store: Create an online store that allows users to browse and purchase products.
10. Image Gallery App: Build an app that displays a collection of images in a grid or slideshow format.
11. Blogging Platform: Create a platform for users to write and publish blog posts.
12. Recipe App: Build an app that allows users to browse and search for recipes.
13. Quiz App: Create a quiz app that asks users multiple choice questions and displays their score.
14. To-Do List with Kanban: Create a Kanban style To-Do list with drag and drop cards to change their status.
15. Contact Book App: Build an app that allows users to save and organize their contact information.
16. Language Learning App: Create an app that teaches users new vocabulary and phrases in a foreign language.
17. Online Marketplace: Build a marketplace app that allows users to buy and sell products.
18. Social Media App: Create a social media platform for users to connect and share content.
19. Video Chat App: Build a video chat app that allows users to communicate in real-time.
20. Workout Tracker App: Create an app that allows users to track their workouts and fitness progress.
21. Task Manager App: Build an app that allows users to manage and prioritize their tasks.
22. Cryptocurrency Tracker App: Create an app that displays real-time information about cryptocurrency prices and trends.
23. News Aggregator App: Build an app that aggregates news

articles from multiple sources.
24. Online Forum: Create an online forum where users can discuss various topics.
25. Fitness Challenge App: Build an app that challenges users to complete daily fitness goals.
26. Budget Planner App: Create an app that helps users manage their finances and create budgets.
27. Job Board App: Build an app that allows users to search and apply for job openings.

EPILOGUE

Now that you have reached here, the final goal as always is to implementing what you found to be useful and build a plan for you to carry out that plan and achieve your vision, the truth is that, it all starts with a vision, a dream and to dig deep in the dirt to make things happen.

AFTERWORD

Now that you have reached here, the final goal as always is to implement what you find to be useful and build a plan for you to carry out that plan and achieve your vision. The truth is that, it all started with a vision, a dream and having the heart to dig deep in the dirt to make things happen when I entered the tech industry.

I wished I knew how things went about and learned the game easily and increase my performance in the long run. That helplessness was something I did not want others to face, so that served as the north star whilst writing the book, to make sure the next generation after the generation that comes after me is greater, smarter and more capable than ever.

ACKNOWLEDGEMENT

This book would never have been possible with the help of tons of individuals who have guided me and loved me to let me take more risks than ever. First of my mom, dad, amachi and both my brothers, they stand at the core of all that I have.

Sujith bhaiya for bringing such a wonderful opportunity to me, without which none of this would have been possible, Deepak Dhanraj, my HR, who was wonderful enough to get me aboard after multiple failures, and gave me another chance to prove myself. My team at Maersk, whose kindness
and support even after multiple failures became a core component in me being a better engineer.

To the reader, friends and people who have supported me unconditionally over the years, to make my dreams a reality and be able to bring life to my goals, which has been able to further serve more people, which has made society better all together.

ABOUT THE AUTHOR

Richu Biju

Richu is an engineer- entrepreneur mix for the modern world and has been someone who has commited his focus to serve as many individuals across the world through his passion and weakness in the tech industry.You can always Richu saying, "Keep punching my friend".

BOOKS BY THIS AUTHOR

Podcasting For Life: Serving A Billion People

As the world becomes more connected and more social, the baseline noise around us increases, and it becomes difficult to put forth your opinions; your demand to be heard is reduced as the world races ahead.

Podcasting gives you the ability to put forth your views, get opinions from leaders in their field, and gives you the power to add value to a lot of people's lives.

Uncommon Amongst Uncommon: In My Relentless Pursuit For Excellence

What if?
What if you had a guidebook with the values and internal conversations of a few of the men who have sacrificed their entire life for excellence and getting better regardless of how they feel, and what society channelled them to become,

Balding With Pride

As humans have grown into the big civilization that it is today, it came at a price, and the price for the prize was the best resource utilisation and passing of genetics. So, naturally, the best of everything gets promoted while the rest decays, so how can you make the most of life's worst gifts?

THE BOOK END HERE FOR NOW

Part 2: Loading

Ingram Content Group UK Ltd.
Milton Keynes UK
UKHW020216250523
422303UK00012B/119